This Book Belongs to

Copyright © 2023
make believe ideas ltd
The Wilderness, Berkhamsted, Hertfordshire, HP4 2AZ, UK.
6th Fl., South Bank House, Barrow St., Dublin 4, D04 TR29, Ireland.

All rights reserved. No part of this publication may be reproduced, stored in a retrieval system, or transmitted in any form or by any means, electronic, mechanical, photocopying, recording, or otherwise, or used to train any artificial intelligence technologies without the prior written permission of the copyright owner.

enquiries@makebelieveideas.com
www.makebelieveideas.co.uk

Written by Annie Simpson.
Illustrated by Ian Worrall-Dutton.

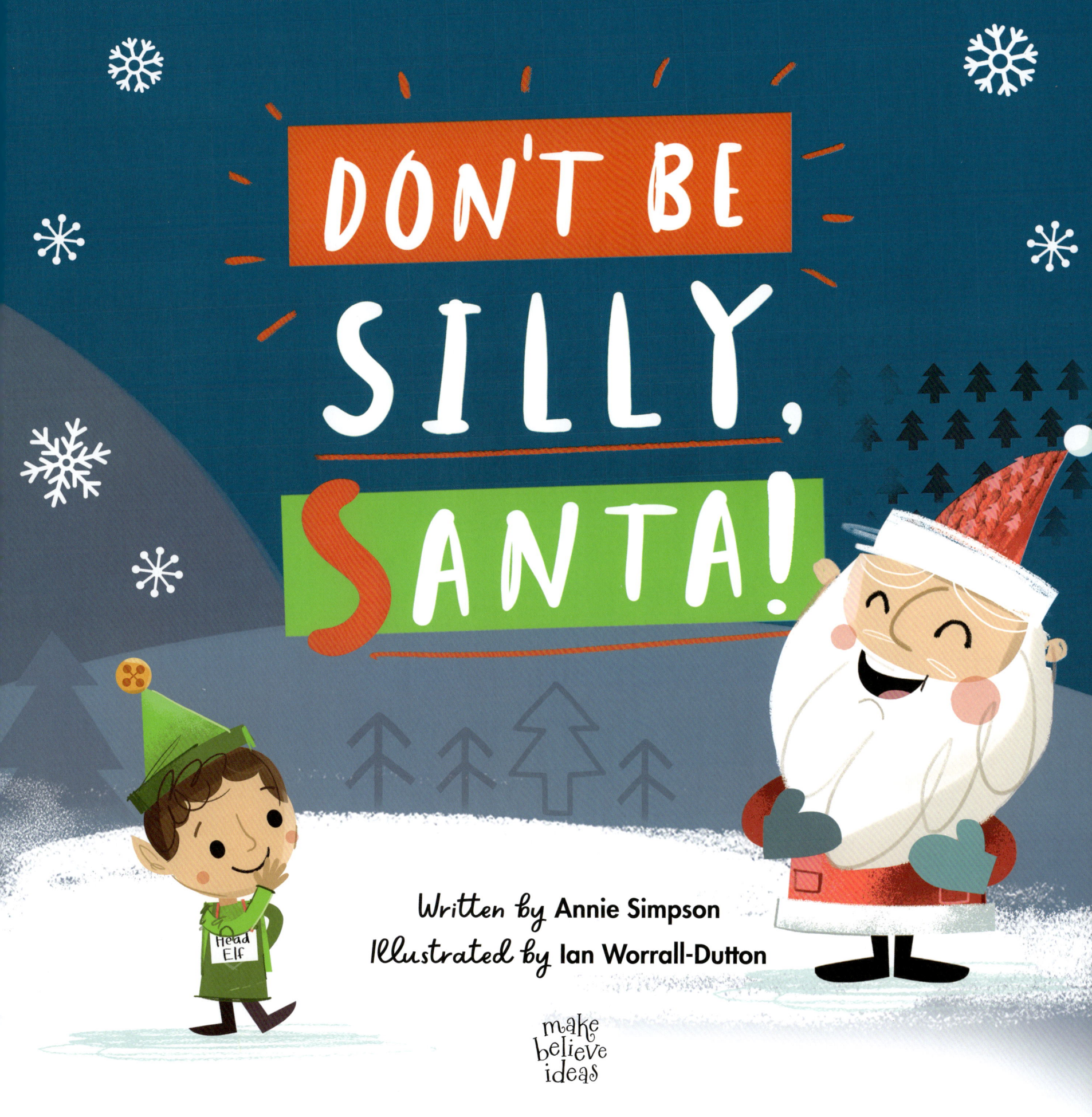

First **check** is the WORKSHOP. Look at all these **toys**!
There's something here for **everyone** – all good girls and boys.

Here's a train ... a car ... a ball ...

a robot dog that **glows**,

There's something **you** should know …

If you keep *interrupting,* on the **Naughty List** YOU'LL GO!

Next up, we have FLIGHT CONTROL.
Snowfall levels are *low*.
How's the **Sleigh Port** looking?
Reindeer set to go?

We're trying to **concentrate**.

If you keep saying *cheeky* things,

you're going to make us

LATE!

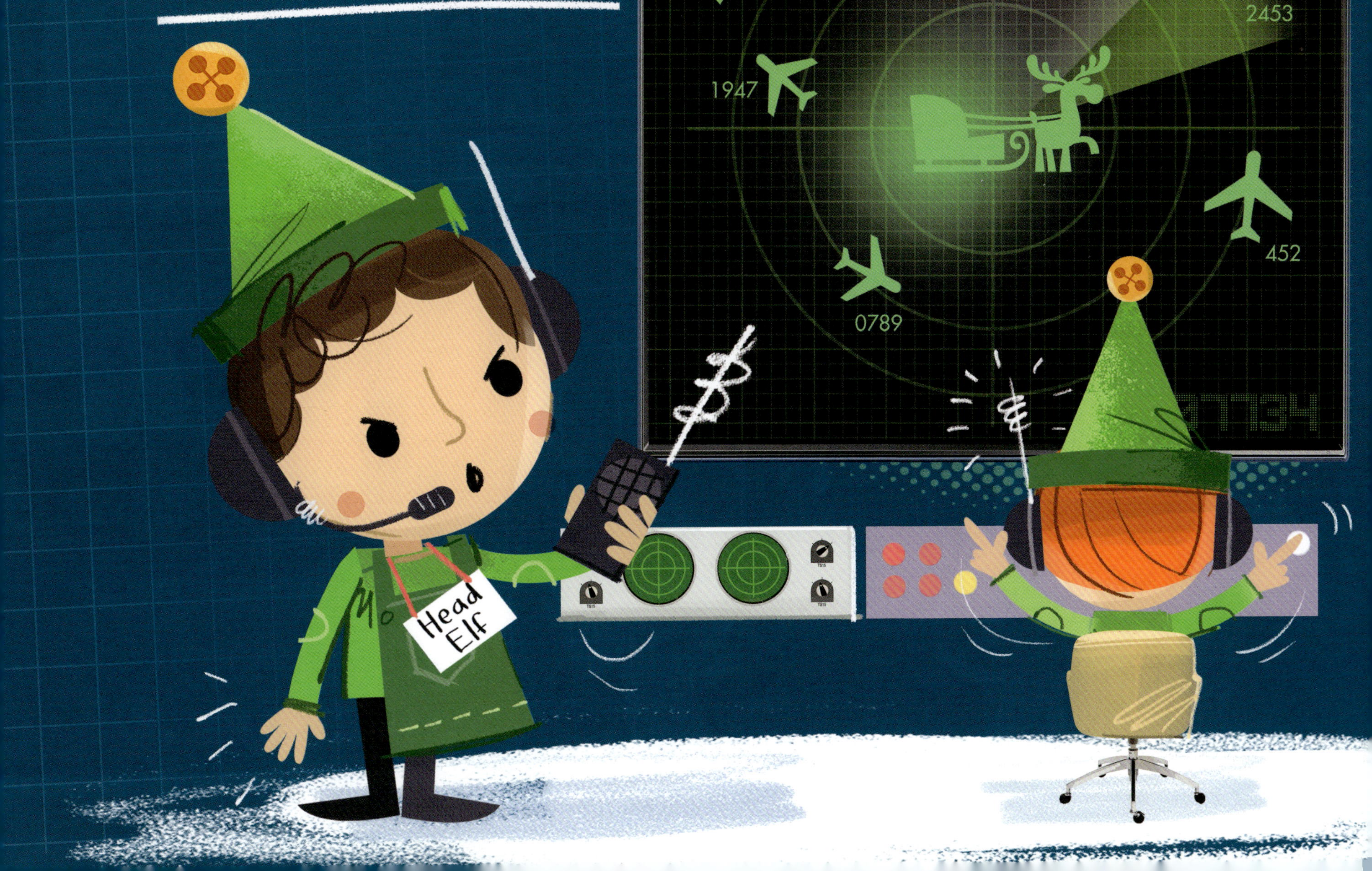
COUNTDOWN CLOCK
10:29
1325
2453
1947
452
0789
Head Elf

Last stop is the WRAPPING CREW – they end our checks tonight. These busy elves make sure the presents always look **just right**.

Finally, **Head Elf** realised Santa was only having *fun* and thought he'd get his own back now that all the work was done.

So, this time it was Head Elf who had something *silly* to say:

"Santa, the reindeer are poorly – you'll have to pull the sleigh!"

Santa was so shocked, his "**Ho, ho, ho!**" became

OH NO!

Everything is ruined, and it's nearly time **to go.**

Head Elf saw that being silly had brought them *Christmas cheer* and decided to put **silliness** on the *checklist* for next year!